# Introduction

## *Your Aims When Teaching Swimming*

- Safety
- Independence
- Watermanship
- Fun
- Good strokes

- and the chance to go on to
    - Life Saving
    - Water polo
    - Synchronised swimming
    - Diving
    - Competition

### *Pupils with a disability*

- As far as possible, pupils with a disability should be taught in the same way as the rest of the class.

- The teacher should expect to use more teaching aids

- ... and be ready to repeat the basic practices for longer.

# Contents

# Safety and Discipline

### *Control*

• The teacher must be in **control**. Accidents often happen because of poor organisation. Prepare thoroughly and think ahead.

• You must be able to **clear the water** within seconds in an emergency.

• **Horseplay** in the changing rooms or on the poolside is particularly dangerous due to the wet floors. Insist that pupils change quietly, do not run, and keep well away from the edge of the pool.

### *Equipment*

• Know where the **first aid** kit is kept. Better still, have a small one with you. Do you have a first aid qualification? Are you up-to-date?

• You should have easy access to a **telephone**. However it may be coin operated. Do you have the correct change?

• **Good housekeeping.** Equipment must be put away when not in use. Loose floats can be very dangerous and must be stored. Pupils should learn that if they use something they should put it away.

### *Swimming wear*

• **Goggles** should only be allowed when chemicals are a problem, or for medical reasons. As swimming teachers it is our job to teach pupils to use their eyes; thus preparing them for future skills such as diving and survival. After all, probably no more than 10mins is spent with the face in the water in an average lesson. And they would not be wearing goggles if they fell into a river or out of a boat!

• **Jewellery** should generally be removed, to avoid scratching others, catching fingers etc. Religious jewellery should be taped down with surgical tape, and bracelets covered with tennis-type sweatbands.

• **A cap** should be worn if hair can get in the eyes.

### *Medical problems and special needs*

- Ensure that any pupil's **medication** (e.g. inhaler) is taken to the poolside.
- Children who suffer from diabetes, epilepsy or ear problems need medical clearance before swimming.
- If a pupil has a special need, it should be defined in writing, and medical and parental clearance to swim obtained.

### *School Travel*

- Know your insurance. Travel with a completed register, making a head count before you leave school, and before you leave the pool premises.

### *Finally ...*

Remember you must be in control of the whole group, *all* the time. They must see this in your attitude. This book is full of positive messages that should keep pupils focused, but sometimes this is not enough. You should mentally rehearse what to do if pupils misbehave - for example if they don't listen, behave badly in the changing room, push one another about on the poolside etc. *Be ready before it happens!*

# Being an Effective Teacher ...

***Dress*** in smart sports-style clothes, not as if you've just come off the beach.

***Behaviour.*** At the first lesson, set a code of behaviour for:

- ***Discipline*** e.g. "When I'm talking, stand still", "When I blow the whistle, I want you out of the water in 10 sec.", etc.
- ***Hygiene*** "Go to the toilet before swimming", "Have a shower" etc.
- ***Safety*** "Stand well back from the edge", "Enter the water only when I tell you to", "Climb out at the nearest side when I give this signal" etc.

***Routine.*** Keep to a routine. Children like to know, for example:

- Where they should stand
- The aim of the lesson. This motivates your pupils.
- How they are going to warm up - at what speed and why.

***Starting the lesson.*** The way in which you start the lesson is vital -

- A confident and reassuring manner
- Positive and clear instructions: "You are going to jump onto the black line, and travel to the other side. Ready ... Jump!"

***Your voice.*** Your voice affects your pupils the very minute you speak.

Practice speaking in a voice that combines authority, enthusiasm and goodwill. If you sense distress, be careful not to allow sympathy to replace the authority. Above all, let your confidence be seen as well as heard.

*Research has shown communication to be -*

| | |
|---|---|
| *Body Language* | *60%* |
| *Tone of voice* | *25%* |
| *Words used* | *15% only* |

Swimming pool acoustics can be terrible. If you don't want to lose your voice completely, you need to use it effectively -

- Stand at the *end* of the line of pupils.
- Make sure you can see all their faces, and they can all see yours.
- *Wait* for their full attention before you speak.
- Speak to the *far end* of the line, so they can all hear you. *Check* that they can all hear you.
- PAUSE
- Action

***Develop skills*** in a regular way:

First teach the skill, and encourage them to perfect it on their own.
Then develop the skill by working with a partner, giving them problem-solving exercises.
Finally put them into small groups, and develop the skill further.

***New work.*** Only advance to new work when the previous skills are done well, and all movements performed with precision. Some pupils may need much repetition before good habits are ingrained -

***PROGRESSIVE PRACTICES***

***PROGRESSIVE CHANGE***

***PERMANENCE***

***SUCCESS***

Look out for good things, and ***praise often*** -

***Set goals*** (attainment targets) and assess against these regularly -

- Short term goals - half termly (every 6 - 7 weeks)
- Longer term goals - by the end of the year.

# Psychology of the Non-Swimmer

*Some children are frightened of going swimming, for a variety of reasons. These include their family's attitude to water, and other factors. Whatever the reason, some children just don't want to get in, and the swimming teacher has to deal with them. Water can be life threatening, but would-be swimmers must confront it and explore it. We must encourage them to do this.*

The swimming environment should be

**• Safe • Enjoyable • Attractive**

## *Fear and Anxiety*

There is nothing wrong with being afraid, but there is no need to stay that way. Almost everyone is afraid of new and different things. Fear is a miserable feeling, sometimes the result of a truly bad experience, but often due to thoughtless conversation, lack of knowledge and 'old wives tales'.

*"Once I nearly drowned. Somebody pushed me in and I fell to the bottom".*

Children are not born afraid of the water, but they *are* born with a fear of falling, so plan the first activities so there will be no feelings of falling, dropping, or bouncing.

They need to learn that the water, no matter how deep, will support them if they will let it!

An apprehensive child will not believe that the depth of the water makes no difference to floating or sinking. Telling them that they swim in the top 2 feet makes no difference. And nothing upsets a frightened child more than the turbulence caused by other swimmers. Some pupils are not afraid - they just don't like having their faces wet. Ideally, of course, preparation for swimming will have started at home!

One of the ways to help them overcome their fear is to provide a controlled environment, where they can sense that someone is looking after them, and generally is in charge. They will feel protected against unknown threats and dangers - and they will feel more secure, relaxed and confident. They want you to be in charge.

### *Setting the ground rules*

The first time you meet with a group, explain that there are a few rules that every one must obey. You need to develop your own list, but they could include:

- "You must all stand well back from the pool side when you come in."
- "You must wait for permission to get into the water."
- "When the whistle blows, go to the nearest side and climb out. Can you be out in ..... *ten* seconds?"

# Psychology of the Non-Swimmer

## *Dealing with a timid pupil*

Outwardly calm

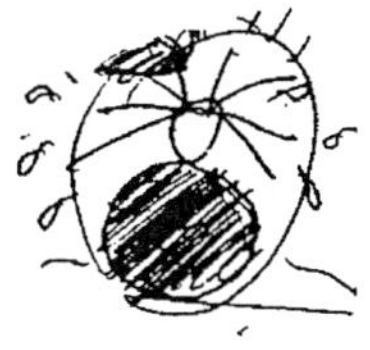

Obviously frightened!

A pupil who shows outward calm is often accepted as confident and 'at home' in the water, but inwardly may be extremely tense and far more fearful than the obviously frightened type. *You must be able to recognise this. An empathetic approach (i.e. putting yourself in their shoes) is important - after all we have all been frightened at some time in our lives.*

- Be prepared to listen. Let them tell you why they are frightened - they will be happier knowing you know!
- Increase their safety and confidence by using teaching aids (armbands etc.).
- When they first get in, let them explore. Give them a feeling of not being watched. (This will take the pressure off.)
- Give reasons why you want them to do things – non-swimmers have brains too!
- Give them things they can almost certainly manage. You should expect at least a 90% success rate for each activity

## *Knowing when to back down*

Waging war is no way to produce confident swimmers -

- Be alert to body language. Once you see a look of refusal, try to avoid a showdown - unless you want one and are ready for it! Change the activity before they protest more loudly.
- Give them a choice - they do either this or that. Be sure both options are within their grasp

*... and finally, for the very rebellious, who refuse to bring kit, you can always make them Equipment Monitor!:*

# Demonstrations

*Children are master imitators - they learn most of their life skills by imitation. When they see something being done, they believe it is possible and want to try it - a useful first step to acquiring a new skill.*

"Can you see the long neck?
"See how the body is stretched like a plank of wood"


Just as "a picture is worth a thousand words", a demonstration is more effective than a lot of verbals. If you see a pupil performing well, get the rest of the class out to watch. They will benefit greatly. Demonstrations also reinforce your teaching points:

There's often a lot going on in a demonstration, and they may focus on the wrong thing, so simplify it as far as possible. Ideally it should show only the point being made.

### *Demonstration tips*

- Ensure the demonstration is spot-on. The class will copy what they have seen, good and bad.
- Demonstrate only the point being made.

- Get the pupils out of the water. They need to look down to see what is happening below the surface.
- Ensure the most distant pupil can hear you. See and be seen by all.
- Keep it simple. Give short, clear teaching points.

- If you are giving a demonstration on the poolside, make sure your action is correct. As you need to keep eye contact with them, you will need to "mirror" the movement.
- Always face the direction the pupils are going to swim

- ... and make sure you don't demonstrate swimming into a wall!

### *Final thoughts on demonstrations*

- Children mirror *moods* as well as actions. They will copy your state of mind as well as your demonstration!

- If you tell them you're going to pick the best and have them show the rest of the group, make sure you do. Otherwise it's a dreadful letdown.

- Remember that a demonstration only makes them believe that the skill is possible. They won't be competent until they do it themselves. So ensure they practice the skill immediately afterwards, otherwise they won't retain it.

- "Tell me, and I forget. Show me, and I believe. I do, and I know."

Of course, some teachers like giving explanations -

# Grouping

*For many reasons, pupils progress at different rates, and the best results come when pupils work with others of similar ability. They are more motivated in a peer group, with aspirations to be 'promoted'.. It is also much easier to teach them.*

Two examples of grouping follow – 'Differentiation' and 'Accelerated Learning'.

### *Differentiation*

This requires groups of differing ability, working at the same skill (e.g. legs only), but at different stages.

- Assess the pupils and group them, keeping the weakest nearest to you for reassurance.
- Give each group a different 'Start' practice, and have each group progress at their own rate. (The strongest group could be several steps ahead of the weakest after a while.)

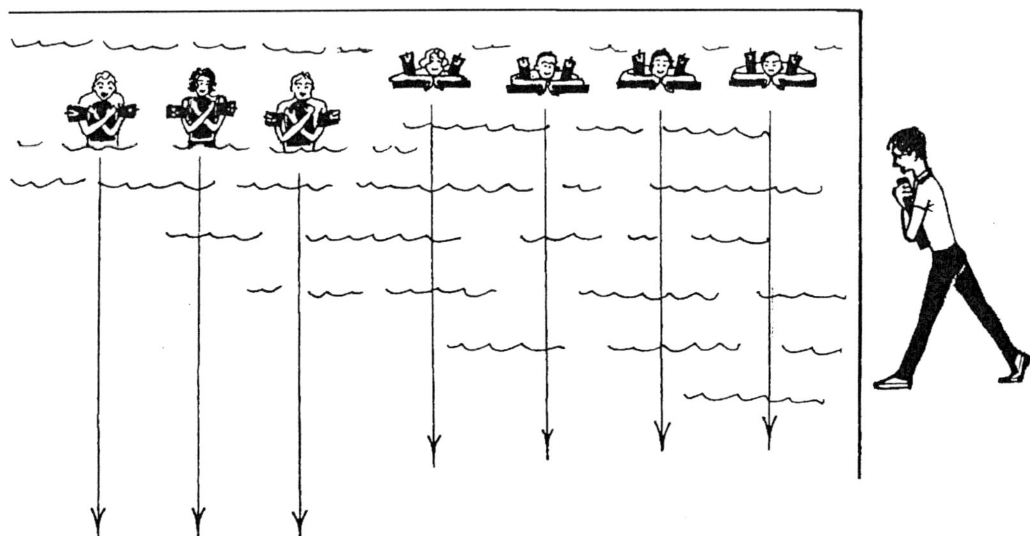

## *Accelerated learning*

For very large classes, lack of space can make grouping difficult. Instead, you can let each pupil decide for him or herself when they are ready to move on to the next practice -

***Method:***

1. Select a number of 'leaders', who can understand and follow instructions well.
2. Organise the class into lines, each behind a 'leader'. The most apprehensive or weakest pupils should be nearest you.
3. Number them off down the lines; each leader is no.1, child behind is no.2 etc.
4. Pick a starting practice e.g. legs only - two floats (the same for everyone), and set them off: "No.1's - Go, No.2's - Go" etc.
5. Repeat this until each child has swum twice.

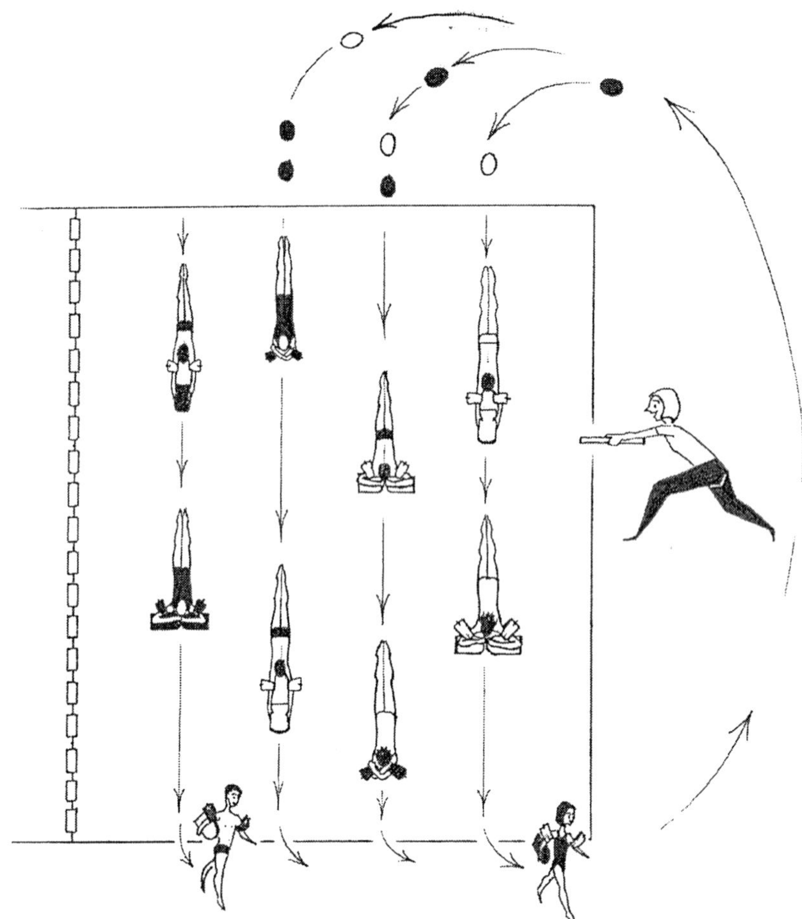

When all are back in their lines, ask them how they got on. E.g. *"Who managed to get across without touching the floor each time? If you did, move your float to ..."* i.e. move on to the next stage. You will now have some with two floats and others with one. Continue progressing and self-checking until they reach the final practice.

# Teaching Aids

*If a teaching aid produces the desired result quickly, it should be used. Nothing succeeds like success Teaching aids are of great value to pupils with a disability.*

## *Arm bands*

### *Advantages*

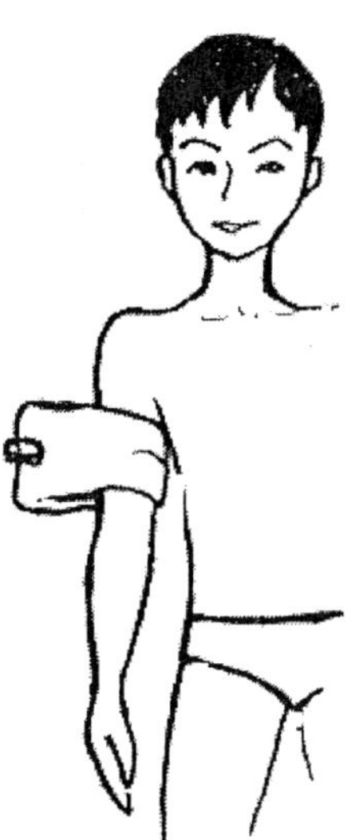

- Enhances pupils' safety, so you can have a large group in the water with confidence.
- Gives them independence from the start, and allows them to warm up.
- Enables them to swim out of their depth - good for large groups.
- Makes for a more active lesson.
- Enables pupils to get into a good swimming position and concentrate on technique.
- Gives them the opportunity to co-ordinate arms and legs, e.g. in front paddle (dog paddle) and breaststroke.

Some people do not like using armbands because they think the children will come to rely on them. *This will only happen if we allow it.* In practice, the concluding activity usually involves underwater play, so the armbands will come off then.

## *Swim belts*

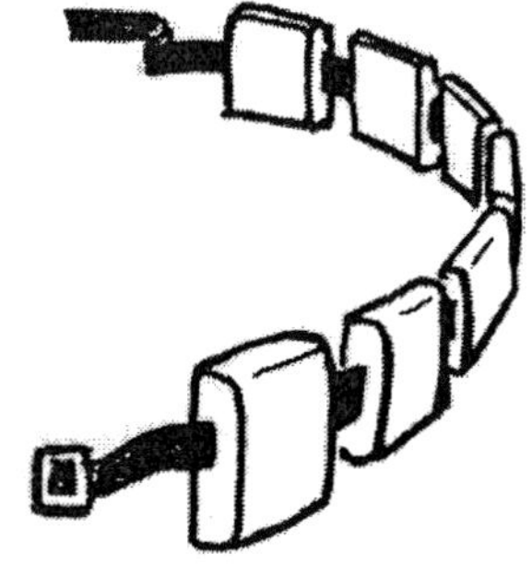

If a pupil is wearing armbands and still walking on the bottom, a swim belt will lift the hips and the feet will then come clear.

## *Floats*

There is no point in making pupils struggle through the water. If the body position is not good they will not make progress.

Floats give support so pupils can concentrate on the teaching points.

Teach your pupils how to use the floats properly - they need to *experience* good support. The way the float is held is very important. If incorrect, they will struggle.

*Wrong* ✗ *Right* ✓

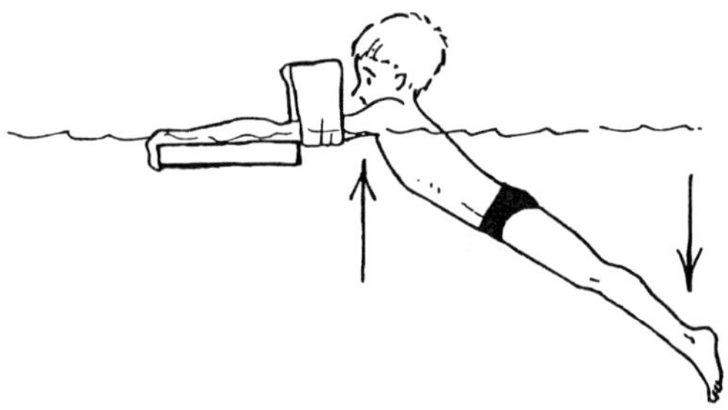

## *The Tuck and Rotation*

They need to tuck in order to rotate. Now is a good time to learn. (When they tuck, they can rotate four times faster.) They will need this skill many times in the future - e.g. -

- for safety in deep water - changing from front to back
- mushroom floats
- somersaults
- handstands
- surface dives
- diving
- tumble turns

Practise the three positions below without a pause, tucking each time they rotate through the sitting position.

"Head forward, chin in the water, and stretch"

- "Press down on your floats"
- "Imagine you are sitting in an armchair"

- "Make your neck long like a giraffe"
- "Show me your stomach!"

### *What if you have no teaching aids?*

You can use these practices if there is no alternative. However, the pupils get no feeling of propulsion, so keep them brief.

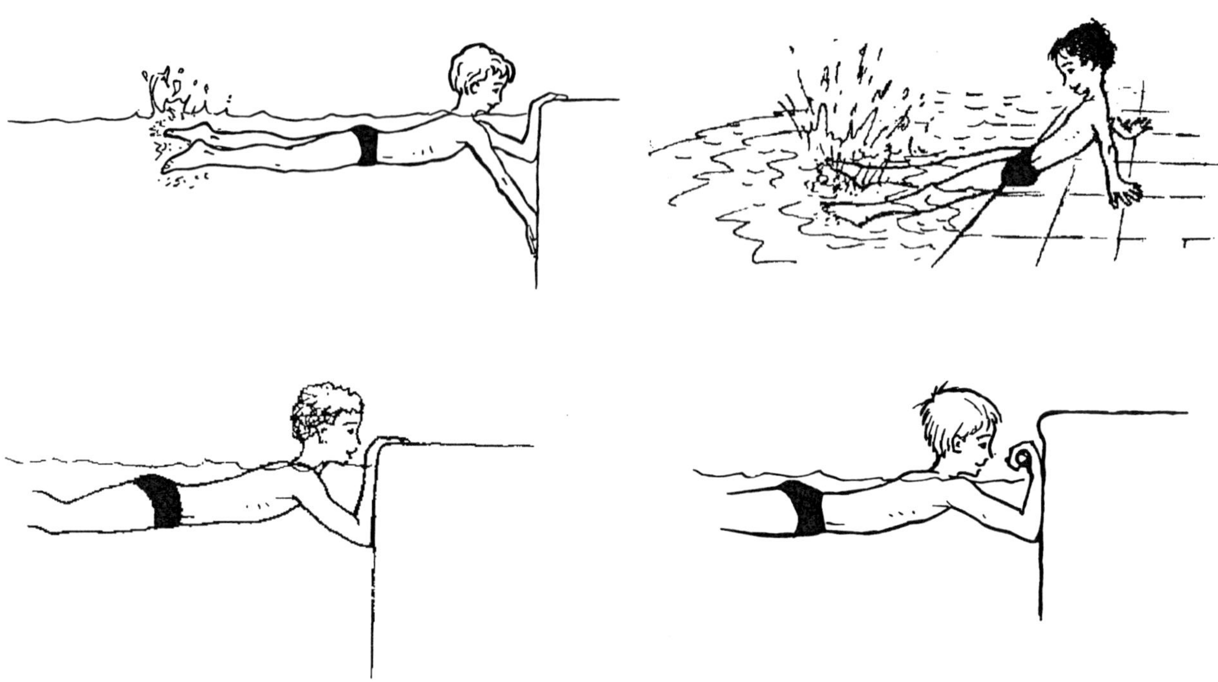

### *Comments ...*

... are almost inevitable when you first introduce teaching aids.

"My Mum says I'm not to wear armbands"

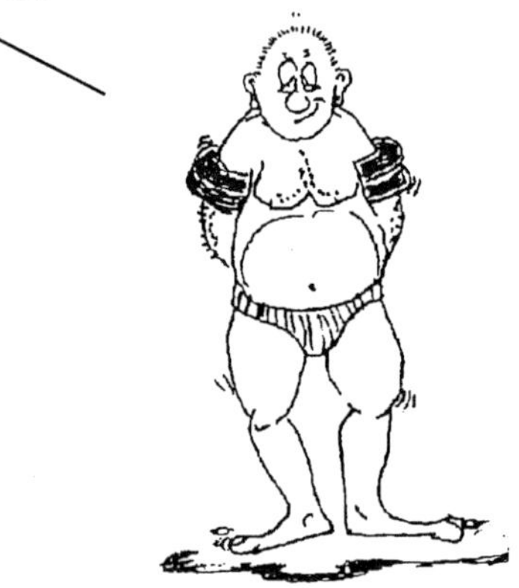

# Body ■ Legs ■ Arms ■ Breathing ■ Timing

*Correct swimming positions are fundamental, and must be taught properly. Long term progress relies on these foundations.*

*It is better for them to do a few strokes well than a lot badly. The maximum distance should be only about 7 metres.*

## *The Body*

***Swimmers should** -*

- be streamlined, like a fish
- be flat in the water, to reduce resistance
- be able to propel themselves straight
- stretch forward, so they get the longest pull with each stroke

***A good body position ...***

- slips through the water
- is a good base from which to introduce the arm actions *when they are ready*

***Body type affects position***

- Fat floats high (think of a cold stew!)
- Muscular types sink
- Bony types sink
- Some just float higher than others

### *Body parts affect position*

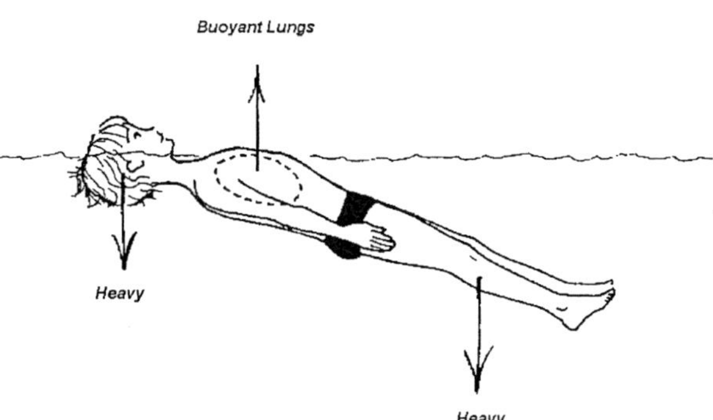


- Not all parts of the body are buoyant!
- and anything out of the water will push you down

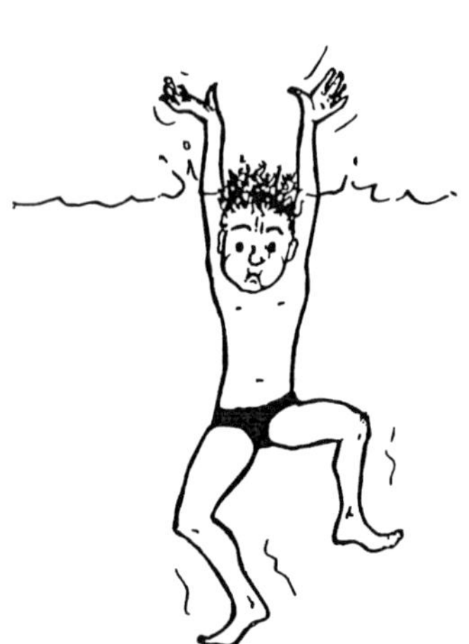

### *Beware dropped hips*

- Dropped hips will increase resistance
- ... and suck you down even further

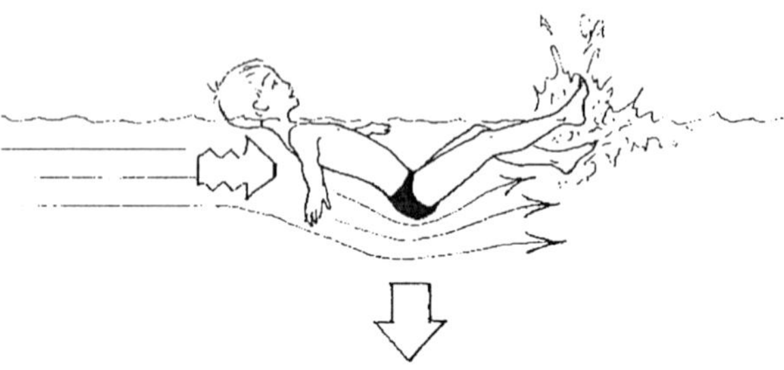

### *The head position*

The head position is crucial as it governs the body position. You can think of it as the 'steering wheel' for the body.

- A high head can be caused by -
  - fear
  - holding the float incorrectly
  - poor breathing technique
  - having to listen to a teacher who talks too much!

- "Keep your chin in the water"

- Keep limbs inside the body width. This reduces resistance.

*Legs*

- Legs stabilise the body, balancing the arms.
- Legs help keep the body in a horizontal position.
- Legs work close together.
- A walking type action (as in crawl) is natural for most people
- ... breaststroke isn't!

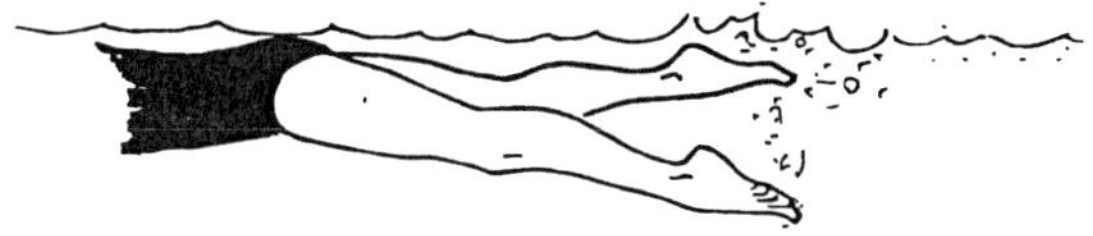

*Arms*

- Arms give the most propulsion, except in breaststroke
- Hands should be placed quietly into the water. 'Noisy hands' means power lost – and you can't beat water into submission!
- Keep arms under the water in the early stages
- Teach them to reach forward to get the longest pull.

- "Watch your hands reach forward like spears
- "How long can you make your spears?"
- "Are they in front of your nose? - or your next door neighbour's?"

### *Breathing*

- Speedboats need a constant supply of petrol. Swimmers need a constant supply of oxygen.
- If you blow out hard, you have more room to take in oxygen.
- Inflated lungs means a buoyant body.
- You never have to tell pupils to breathe in!

### *Timing*

... and if all the foregoing has been taught properly, correct timing will happen automatically.

---

***With constant repetition,***
***precisely practised movements become second nature,***
***like reflexes***

# Entries

*Entries must be safe, with no unpleasant experiences. (Remember that children have an instinctive fear of falling). However, we must eliminate the fear of jumping in as soon as possible. Their confidence will increase dramatically as soon as they can jump in.*

***Teachers should***

- Check the point of entry
- Check the depth of the water
- Make pupils look up to forget the water
- Maintain eye-to-eye contact throughout for reassurance
- Ensure your pupils enter on a given command

## *Jumping in*

***Step One***

- "Hold the hoop with both hands"
- "Bend your knees"
- "Look up – jump up"

***Step Two***

Hold the hoop *just* above arms' reach

- "Look up"
- "Jump up and catch it"

*Step Three*

Hold the hoop higher still

- "Look at the hoop"
- "Jump up and tap the hoop"
- "Bend and spring"
- "How high can you jump?"
- "How far can you jump?"

***Always aim for height and distance***

## *A swivel entry*

Use this -

- if you have a new group and you don't know their ability
- if you need to get a group into the water quickly to practice something

- "Place both your hands to one side of your body"
- "Roll onto your tummy"
- "Slide into the water feet first - like a seal"

## *Backwards*

Use this for -

- the very nervous pupil
- someone with special needs

## *Walking in the water for the first time*

Some pupils will often tiptoe or wobble when walking in the pool for the first time - the resistance acting on the lower part of the body makes it difficult to walk. Also, buoyancy seems to change gravity , and upsets balance.

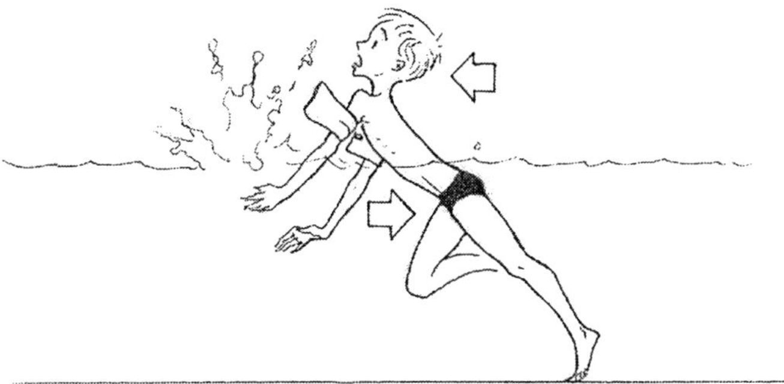

***Remedies -***

- *First* on their own, using the rail. Giant strides with arms outstretched to help balance. Keeping the shoulders under the water will help

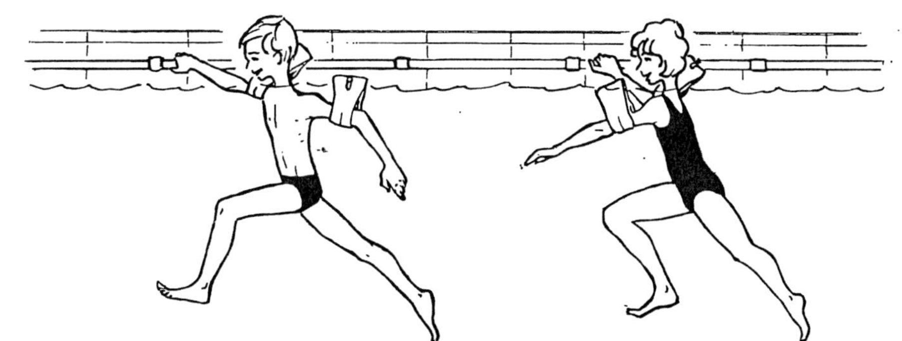

- *Then* play " Little old people" or " Pixies" : hands resting on the shoulders of the person in front in crocodile fashion.

- This can be developed with " Now make the shape of a circle ... (or triangle)" etc.

***Confidence comes from repeated good experiences***

***Progress gradually***

***Learn and practice in a logical order***

# Exits

*Teach your pupils to climb out as soon as possible -*

- *it saves time, as they won't have to queue at the steps*
- *it means that they can get out quickly in an emergency*
- *it gets them ready for exiting deep water*
- *and it strengthens the arms*

***Step One***

"Hands shoulder width apart"

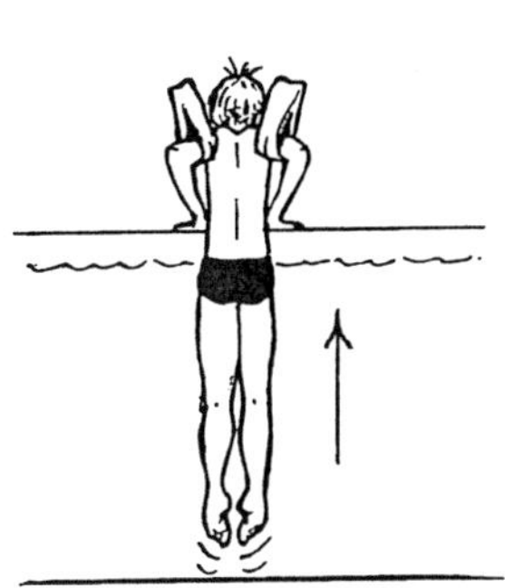

"Jump up"
"Push down"

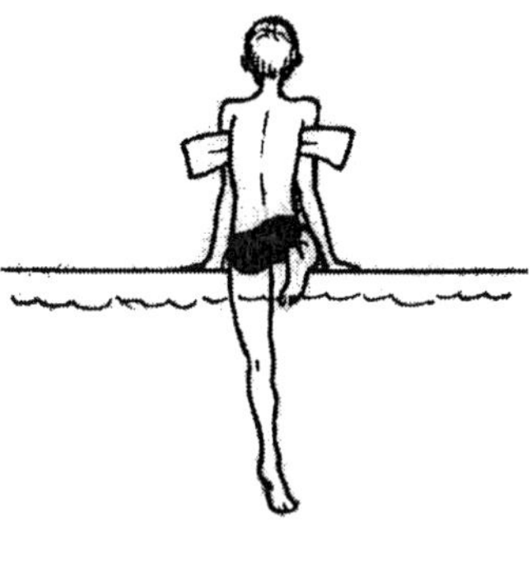

"Lock elbows tight"
"Hold it"

**Repeat the first two positions several times, then the first three several times.**

N.B. If there is a rail, they should use it in the first two positions, then bend forward at the waist onto the side, then push up into position 3.

***Step Two***

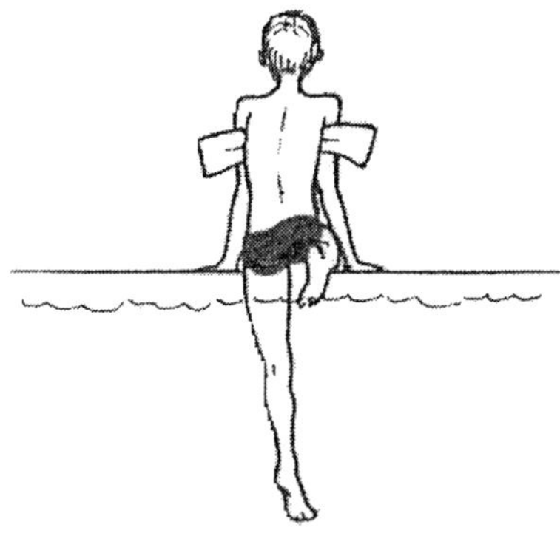

"One knee between your hands"

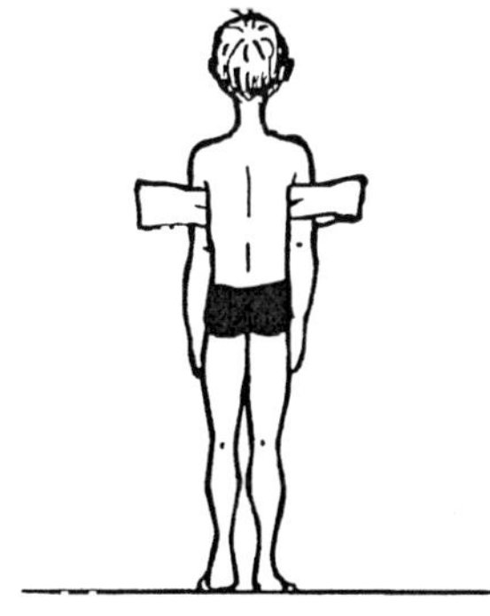

"... and climb out"

"We use muscles, not steps!"

N.B. Children with special needs should try this method before using the steps.

# Propulsion

*To be ready for the following, they should know how to rotate easily from front to back, and be able to regain a standing position quickly from either. If necessary, see the paragraph "Teach your pupils to use floats" (page 20).*

*Swimmers go through many phases, and some are backward. This may be caused by poor co-ordination, but sometimes because basic movements were poorly taught. As always, **foundations must be sound so skills learnt can be transferred to the next stage.***

## *The launch*

Initially, teach movements which do not need the head to go under. They must be able to breathe freely - e.g. back paddle, front paddle, breaststroke.

For each exercise, *the head* must be in a good position before pushing off.

### *On the front*

One foot on the wall behind the hips. This gives a direct thrust through the hips.

- "Chin in the water"
- "Thumbs half way up the float"
- "Push and stretch"

### *On the back*

The foot should be just under the water. This puts it in a direct line with the hips.

- "A long neck like a giraffe"
- "Look at the ceiling."
- (This puts the 'steering wheel' in the correct position before travelling.)
- "A gentle push and stretch"

## Back Paddle

*Two floats*
- Long neck
- Legs under water
- Silent kick

*Float on chest*
- Neck like a giraffe
- Knees under water
- Legs close together

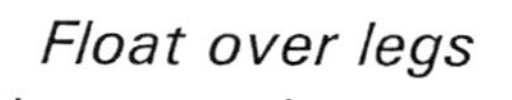

*Float over legs*
- Long neck
- Long legs
- Stretch from head to toe

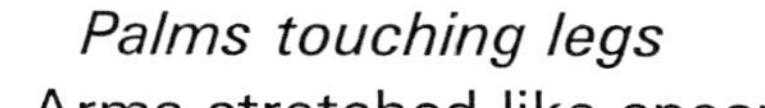

*Palms touching legs*
- Arms stretched like spears
- Silent kick

## Front Paddle (Dog paddle)

*Two floats*
- Knuckles touching
- Chin on hands
- Tiny splash

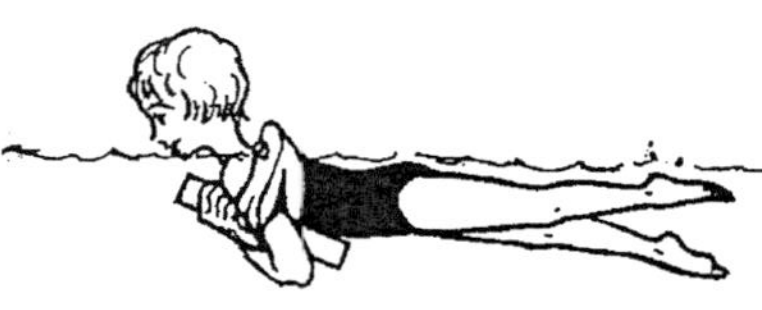

*Float on chest*
- Hug the float tight
- Chin in the water
- Legs close together

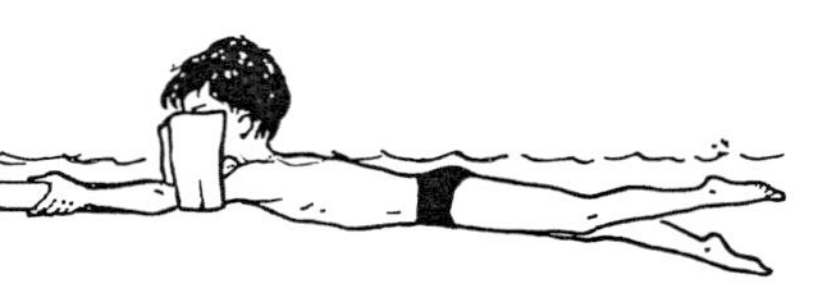

*Float extended*
- Chin in water
- Long arms
- Tiny splash

*Front paddle*
- Hands under water
- Arms like spears
- Reach and pull down

## Propulsion

***Breaststroke.*** *- Some pupils are natural at breaststroke, and will be keen to tackle these practices early. The others should have a go at some stage in their development.*

***Recommended Method -***

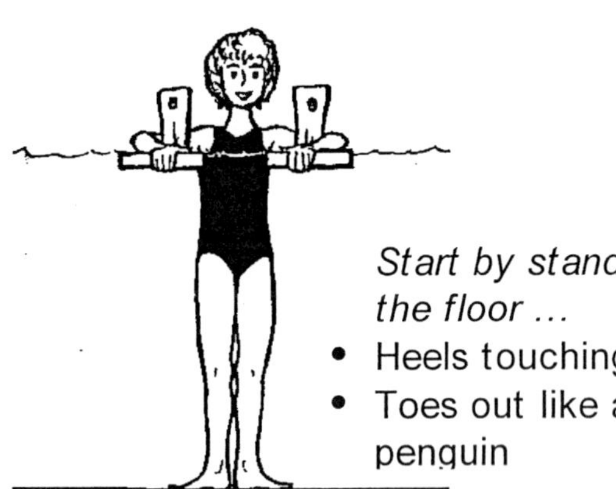

*Start by standing on the floor ...*

- Heels touching
- Toes out like a penguin

*...then vertical ...*

- Heels up to seat (toes out)
- Heels out wide
- Heels back together
- Repeat many times

**... then repeat this sequence, rolling into and out of the middle practice until they can travel forward with a correct foot action ...**

*Lean back*

- Keep the action going
- Heels make circles

*Vertical - (same as top right)*

- Check toes
- Repeat many times

*Lean forward*

- Heels up
- Heels out
- Heels together

*Accelerated Learning can be used to decide when they are ready to progress from this sequence . See page 19.*

**... and finally on to ...**

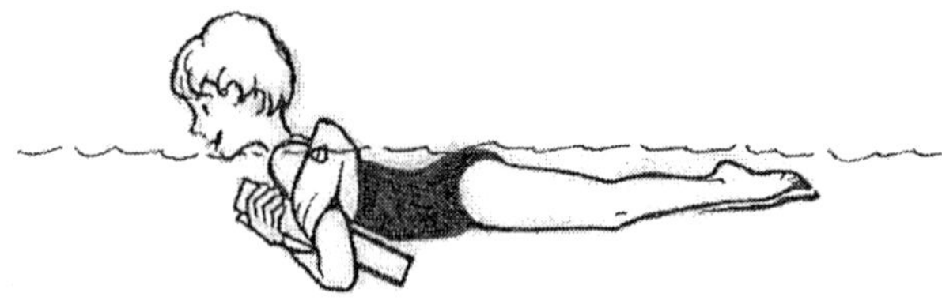

*float on chest ...*

- Hug float
- Chin in water
- Bend, kick and together

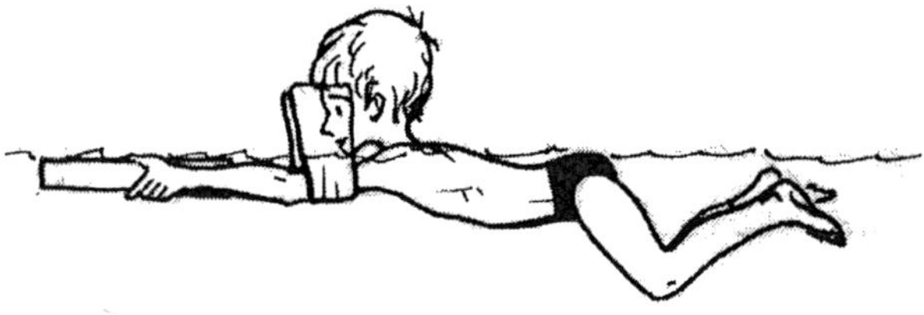

*...and float extended*

- Heels up
- Kick and glide

***Another method in common use -***

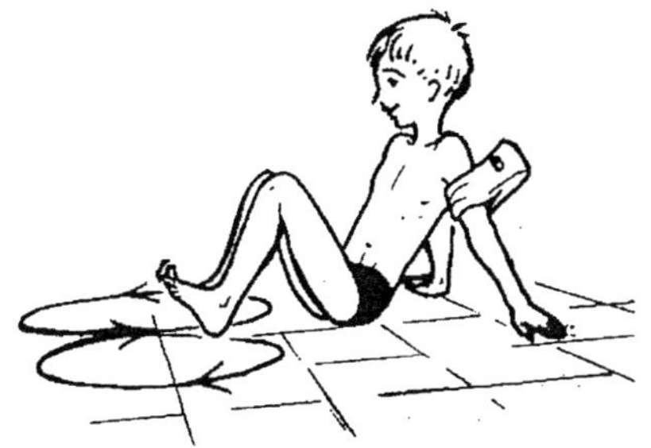

*Sitting on the side*
- Toes curled up
- Heels make circles
- Bend - Out - Together

*Two floats*
- Toes up
- Heels push water away
- Bend - Out - Together

*At the side*
- Heels up to seat
- Turn feet out like a penguin
- Kick back with heels

*Two floats*
- Knuckles touching
- Chin on hands
- Heels up – Out - Together

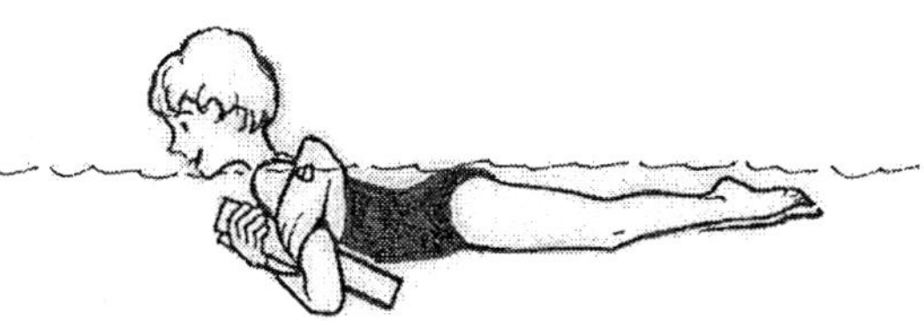

*float on chest ...*
- Hug float
- Chin in water
- Bend, kick and together

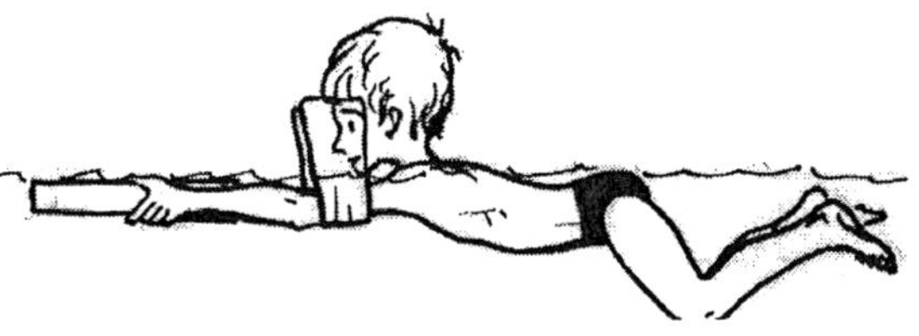

*...and float extended*
- Heels up
- Kick and glide

### *Breaststroke arms*

Once your pupils can travel forward maintaining a reasonable foot action, *then* is the time to add the arm action. If you add the arms before there is power in the legs the pupils will compensate by pulling back too far and wide. This will cause problems with co-ordination and breathing.
To introduce the arms:

- Show very small movements (sculling-type movements) at arms length, in front of the face
- Hands should be touching as they 'spear' their way forward
- Using a 'woggle' under the armpits helps concentration on co-ordination and prevents pulling back too far. The elbows are needed to trap the 'woggle'. This is a very successful method.

---

### *General rule ...*

***Progress each practice until you feel they have reached their limit. There is nothing to be gained from continuing further - they will only develop faults.***

# Removing Arm Bands

*Pupils should be able to travel about 5 metres before you consider total armband removal. And having taught them the basics with armbands, you cannot simply take them both off and say "Off you go!" A step-by-step approach is needed.*

## *On the front*

***Step One:*** **two armbands on.** ***Push and glide to the wall.***

Line the pupils up about one metre away from the wall. Stand facing them so you can demonstrate, and to reassure them.

- *One* metre from the wall
- One foot forward, for balance
- Hands held together
- Chin in the water
- Push and float to the wall

- "Push and stretch"
- "Glue your arms to your ears"
- "Feel your legs float up to the surface"

***Step Two:*** **still two armbands.** ***Adding arms and legs.***

- Move back *two* metres from the wall.
- Swim front paddle to the wall

- "Reach and pull down"
- "Reach for the wall"
- "Reach in front of *your* nose, not your neighbours"

***Step Three: Removing arm bands progressively.***

Repeat the paddle to the wall. Tell them that if they do well, you will ask them to take off one armband.

*Some will now be in two armbands, and some in one.*

Repeat the front paddle to the wall again. Again, those doing well will be asked to take off one armband.

*Some will now be in two, some in one, and some in none.*

N.B. The same teaching points are used throughout.

## *On the back*

***Step One:* Two armbands. *Ready:***

- Hold the rail with both hands
- Feet high on the wall for direct thrust
- Knees on chest
- 'Long neck' to put the head in the correct position

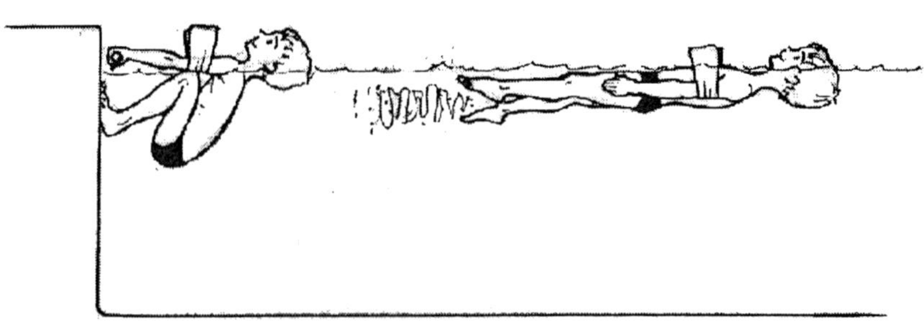

- " Long neck - like a giraffe"
- " Push and stretch"
- " Silent kick"

***Step Two:* One armband -**

Explain that they will feel lopsided. Suggest they *lift* the shoulder of the arm without the armband. (They soon compensate.)

**Ready -** as for Step One

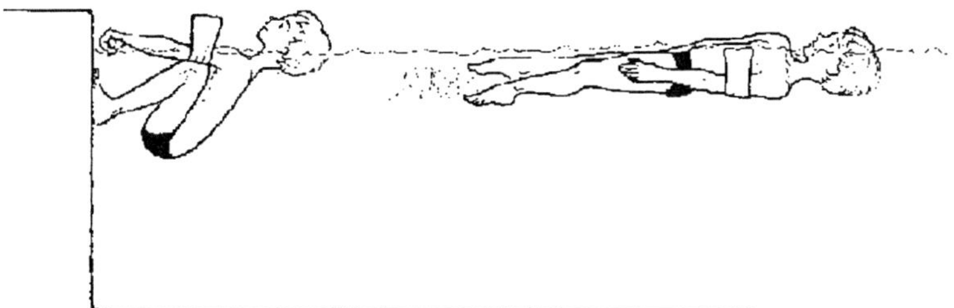

- " Shoulder up"
- " Long neck"
- " Silent kick"

**Step Three: *No arm bands.***

**Ready:** as for Step One -

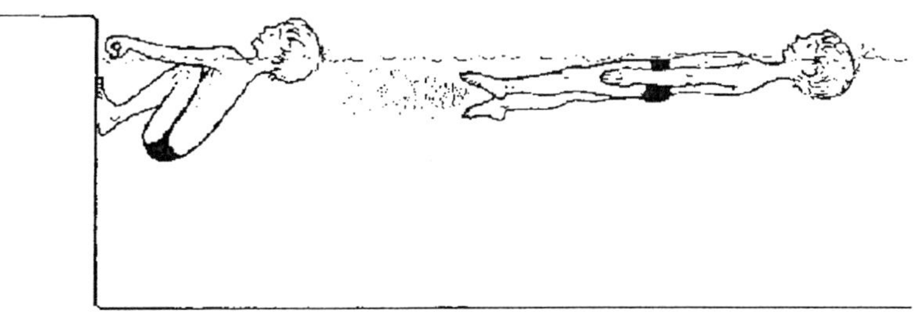

- " Stretch like a sergeant-major"
- " Palms of hands touching your legs"

N.B. They will tend to lift their heads in disbelief - just point to the ceiling.

- Do not talk once they've set off or they will lift their heads to listen to you!
- To swim backwards the head (steering wheel) must be *back* and *still.*

---

***Celebration!*** At the end of the lesson, arrange a small celebration. Get everyone onto to the poolside to watch those who have managed to swim 5 metres without armbands. They've done well, and should get a round of applause. *They are now out of armbands for good.*

# Safe in Deep Water

*To be safe in deep water, pupils must be able to do the following without stress:*

1. *Tread water (the most important skill) for at least 30 seconds, with a 180 degree turn half way through*
2. *Perform safety skills to avoid panic*
3. *Jump confidently into deep water and climb out*
4. *Swim at least 20m on the front* and *on the back*

## *Treading Water*

***Step One: in shallow water at armpit depth.*** **Two floats for support.**

Ready -

- Standing with water at arm pits
- Legs wide as if doing the splits. (This increases resistance and helps them stay up.)
- Hold a float in each hand, elbow resting on it.

- " 30 splits facing one way - 180° turn - 30 splits the other way"
- " How wide can you make your legs"
- " Slow - Wide - Giant strides"

***Step Two - into deep water two floats.***

Ready - *Make sure you have a safety pole in your hand!*

Pupils must -

- face the *end* of the pool. This prevents them drifting out of your reach.
- keep an elbow close to the wall at all times.

- " Imagine you are sitting on an exercise bike"
- " One leg in front and one behind" (except breaststroke)
- " 30 splits one way - Turn - 30 more"

***Step Three - deep water - no floats***

Ready -

- Face the *end* of the pool
- Shoulder close to the wall
- Let the pupil choose one of the leg actions below

" Can you see one leg in front all the time?"

"Who can manage 5 seconds?" ... then 10 etc.

***Step Four - on the poolside at the deep end -***

**Method:**

- Pupil jumps (about 1 metre) and turns to face *the end* of the pool
- 15 sec. treading water one way - turn - 15 sec. the other way
- Swim back to side and climb out

## Safety Skills

*You must be absolutely confident that your pupils are safe in deep water. Don't take chances! In particular, they must be able to tread water properly. Don't introduce these safety skills unless they are ready. Ask them if they think they are ready for deep water.*

- **What to do if frightened.** Ask the pupils to imagine that they have set off across a deep, wide pool and suddenly they become frightened. They panic and start making quick frantic movements. "What will happen?" They will know from treading water that they will sink. You can introduce the following which will help them -

Rotating about a horizontal axis -

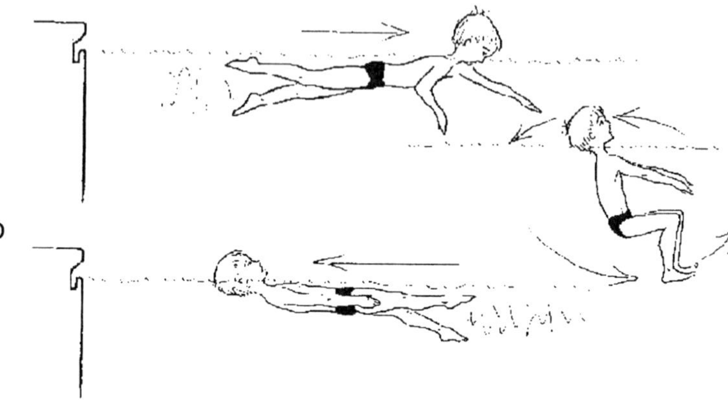

- Travel 5 metres on the front
- Sit up (tuck) - *head back*
- Roll backwards and back paddle to safety

- Travel 5 metres on the back
- Sit up (tuck) - *head forward*
- and swim back to safety

**What to do if tired.** What should they do if they get tired when swimming? Give them this drill -

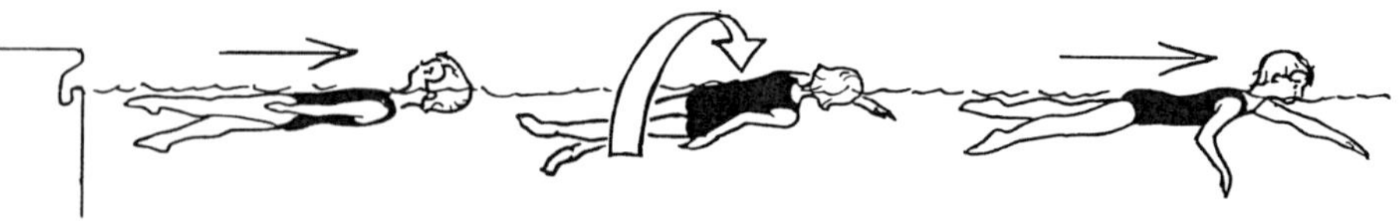

Travel 5 metres on the back, roll over and continue for 5 metres on the front.

# Play With a Purpose

*With children, it's very effective to disguise learning as a game. They are more relaxed, enjoying the fun atmosphere, and leave feeling happy and wanting to return for more.*

*The teacher, however, must not get carried away – remember we're not playing games for their own sake!*

N.B. Arm bands **off!**

**Method:** First teach the skill individually, then let them develop it with a partner

## *Breathing.*

### *Individually*

- "Blow out hard"
- "How many times can you blow the ball over?"

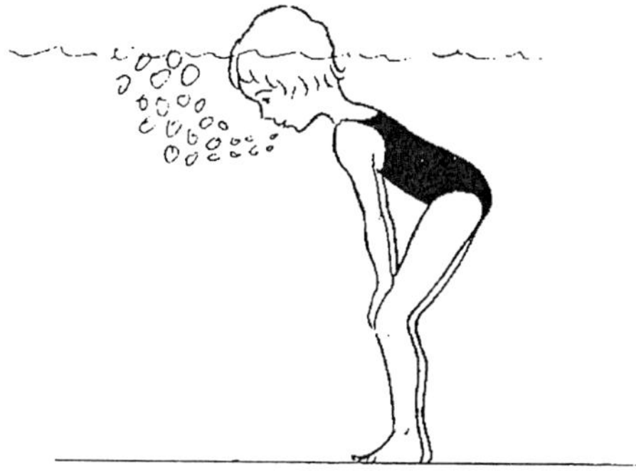

- "How many bubbles can you make?"
- "Who can blow the loudest?"
- "Who can shout their name under water?"

### *Now with a partner*

- "Down and blow"
- "Blow and up"
- "Who can keep going the longest?"

"Jack in the box"

## Submerging

Children will tend to lean forward to pick up an object.. This increases their surface area, and makes submerging almost impossible. If the object is at their <u>*side*</u> they won't do this.

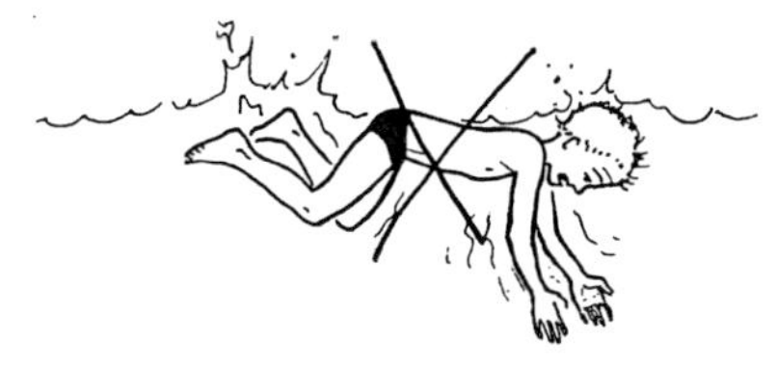

### *Individually*

- Make sure the object is at their side.
- Arms must be close to their sides (to avoid increasing resistance).
- Make sure they jump up high first. (What goes up, must come down).
- "Blow out"
- Following the jump up, the hand should go straight on top of the object

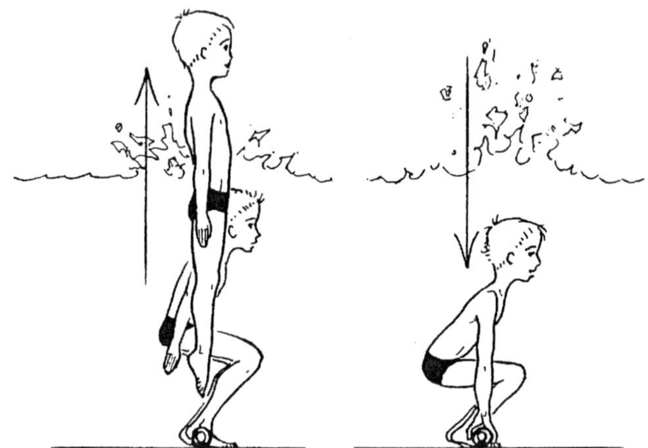

### *Now with a partner ... facing each other*

- "Who can jump high and sit on the floor"
- "How many fingers is your partner holding up?"
- "Can you see your partner smiling?"

## Submerging and rotating

***... with a partner***

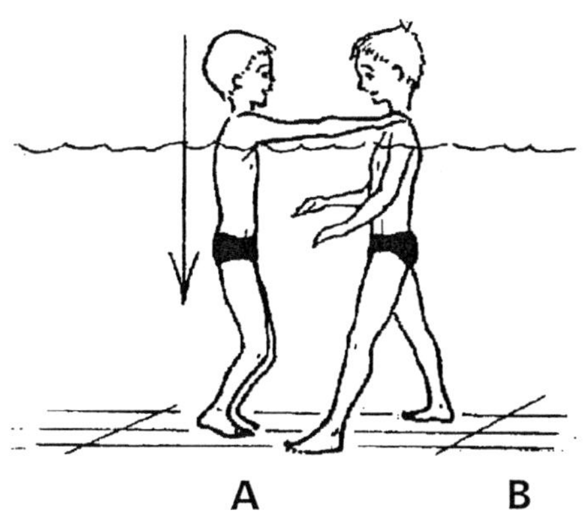


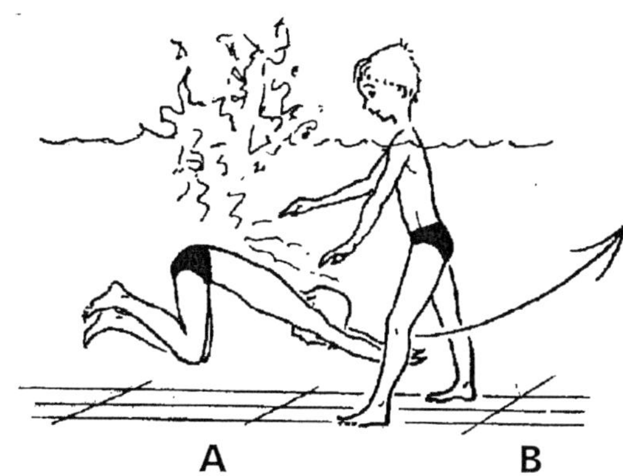


- A, the jumper, places hands on B's shoulders. This keeps them close together.
- B stands with legs wide apart, and ready to help A through.
- A jumps high, sinks *onto knees, rolls forward* and swims through.

***Now develop - as a group. "Through the tunnel"***

Double up and get into fours. Hands on the shoulders of the person in front ...
Ready:

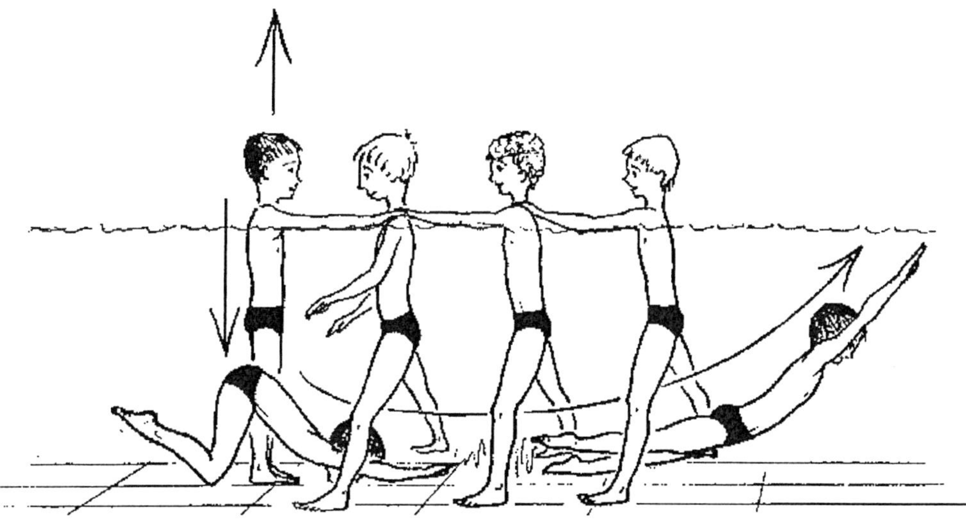

- "Jump high and sink on to your knees"
- "Roll forward to put your chin on the floor"
- "Swim through"
- "Keep your 'steering wheel' close to the floor or you'll bob up again"

## Streamlining

***Individually. Push and glide from the wall***

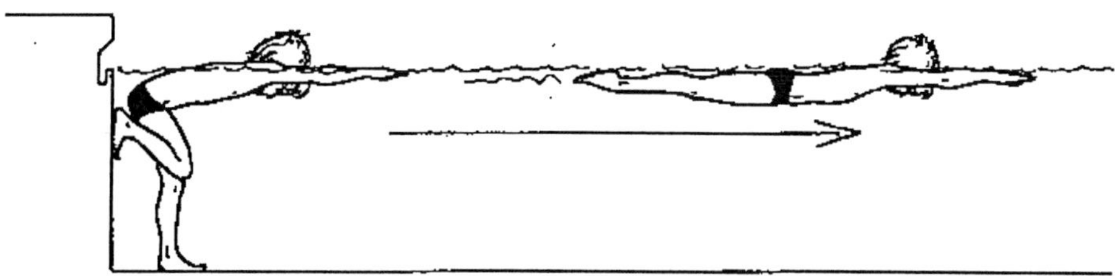

- The foot on the wall should be as near to the seat as possible, to push off straight
- Both eyes in the water, with arms covering the ears, and hands held together. " Squeeze and lock tight." (This skill will be needed many times in the future.)
- Give a vigorous push through the hips.
- " Stretch from finger to toe, *like a spear*"

***With a partner. "Who can glide the furthest?"***

- One partner glides, the other 'marks the spot'.
- The teaching points are the same as 'Individually' above.

***In fours -***

Push and glide from the wall, *down* through the legs and *glide* up to the surface.

- " Tip hands upwards and lift the chin to resurface"
- " Hands together to protect your head"

## Flotation

*Aims: To experience the effects on buoyancy of air in the lungs and the weight of the legs*

***Star float** -*

- Individually -

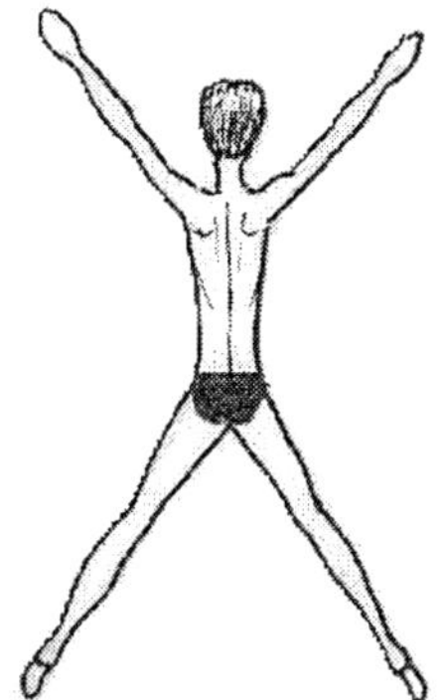

- "Float wide like a star"
- "Face in the water"
- "Pointed toes"

- With a partner -

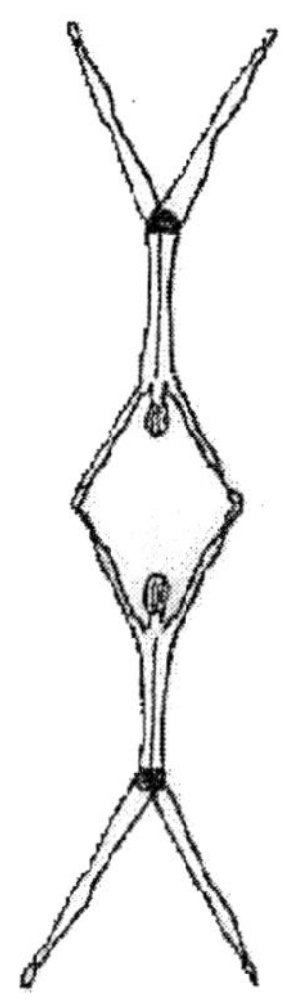

- "Hold hands"
- "Who can float the longest?"

- In fours -

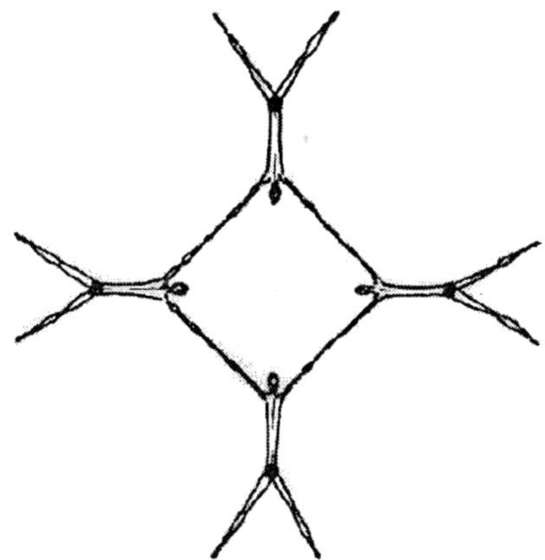

- "Hold hands"
- "On the count of three, everyone floats like a star, face down"
- "What does this remind you of?" (Sky diving)

*Mushroom float*

- Individually -

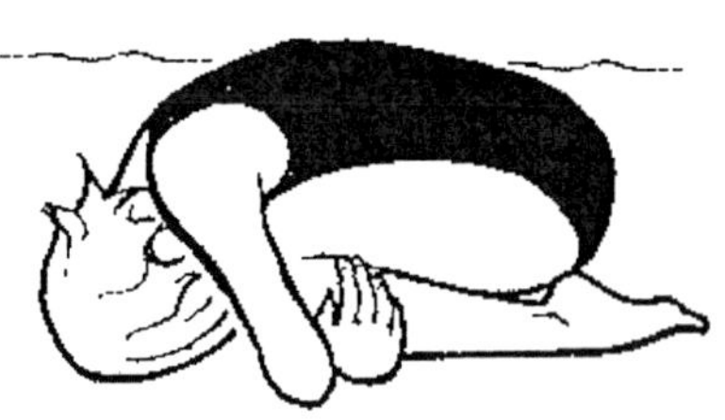

- "Bring your knees to your chin"
- "Curl up like a ball"
- "How small can you make yourself?"
- "Wrap your arms tight round your legs"

- With a partner

Partner ('observer') gives points for -

- Knees touching chin
- Arms wrapped round legs
- Knees and feet together

- Now double up into fours, then six, eight etc. -

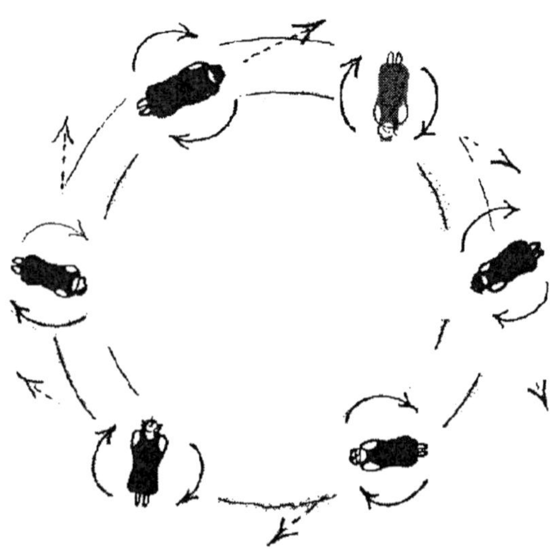

- Pupils hold hands and make a circle
- The circle is made to run round at speed
- At a given signal - "MUSHROOM" - pupils let go and tuck into a mushroom
- Why do the mushrooms spin round?

## Problem Solving

***Which is the easiest way to float?***

Wide like a star?

Thin like a pin?

Small like a ball?

*Why do you think it's the easiest?*

*How can you make a mushroom sink?*

***Get into small groups, hold hands and make the shape of a -***

- circle
- oblong (rectangle)
- square
- triangle

***Get into threes, hold hands and make a triangle***

How many ways can you find to turn the triangle inside out without letting go?

*Aim: getting faces wet!*

## *Academic reinforcement*

*The very young, and those with learning difficulties, sometimes find it hard to concentrate well enough to understand complex instructions. Using familiar objects can help.*

Objects could be:

- floating or sinking
- coloured
- numbered
- lettered

These are easily made from yoghurt cartons and coloured with waterproof pens.

***Step One*** Hold up a (e.g.) yellow object, and ask them to find that colour. E.g. "Who will be the first to bring me a yellow object?" (Show the object throughout the exercise.)

***Step Two*** Do not show the colour. *"Who will be the first to bring me something yellow?"*

***Step Three*** (to take place after all the colours have been gone through.) "Who can bring me a yellow object *and* a blue object?"

***Step Four*** ...then extend to three colours, then four.

***Further Development …***

- Hold up a card. Ask them to find a letter to make a word …

c a __

- … then hide the card and ask them to find letters to make a new word

- Similarly with numbers …

4 + 2 = __

Remember it is not the intention to teach Maths and English, but just a ruse to take their minds off the water. Keep each exercise simple. (However, if they are pre-school children, their parents will love it!)

## *Other games …*

| | *Aim* |
|---|---|
| ❖ Jump high and touch the roof | Spring & Stretch |
| ❖ Jump high and spin like a helicopter | Spring and Rotate |
| ❖ Jump high then *kneel* on the floor | Height & Submerge |
| ❖ Jump high then *sit* on the floor | Height & Submerge |
| ❖ Jump high and touch the floor with one *elbow* (or both) | Rotate |
| ❖ Jump high and touch the floor with your *chin* | Rotate |
| ❖ Jump high and touch the floor with your *ear* | Rotate |
| ❖ Spin round like a ball | Float & Rotate |
| ❖ Kick like a frog | Propulsion |
| ❖ Feet like a penguin | Propulsion |
| ❖ Kick as if a motor boat | Propulsion |

## *Music ...*

Get them into a circle. Find a space.

There are many songs which can be used to disguise your aims. Music is very effective at taking their minds off water. For example:

*To the tune of "If you're happy and you know it"*

| | *Aim* |
|---|---|
| ❖ "Clap your hands (above your head") | Develops balance |
| ❖ "Blow out bubbles" | Introduce breathing |
| ❖ "Splash a friend" | Get used to water in the face |
| ❖ "Disappear" | Submerging |
| ❖ "Jump up high" | Stretch ready for submerging |
| ❖ "Turn around" | Body awareness |
| ❖ "Sit on the floor" | Submerging |
| ❖ "Float like a ball" | Flotation |

*To the tune of "The wheels on the bus go round and round ..."*

- ❖ "The children on the bus go up and down ..."
- ❖ "The wipers on the bus go swish, swish, swish ..."

- ❖ "Bouncing balls go up and down
  Up and down
  Up and down
  Bouncing balls go up and down
  All day long.

  Bounce bounce this-away
  Bounce bounce that-away
  All day long."

*Do The Conga, in a chain following the leader -*

"Hiya hiya conga, conga, conga ..."

# Reciprocal Teaching

'Reciprocal teaching' allows your pupils to take responsibilities for their own learning -

1. Teach the basic skill

2. Pupils work in pairs and follow guidance - this could be given verbally or via a worksheet

***Method -***

- One 'teaches', the other performs.
- Tell the 'teacher' what to look for - e.g. one point if the arms are tightly round the legs, one point if the chin is on the knees.
- The 'teacher' tells their partner how many points they've got
- and what was good
- ... and how to make it better.
- They then change roles.

***Advantages of this method***

- Pupils are fully engaged in the learning process.
- Pupils are encouraged to think why and how things happen.
- By analysing their partner's efforts, they think more about their own.
- They are keen to work hard for one another.
- Personal and social skills are practised.
- The atmosphere is stimulating and happy.
- The teacher is free to observe and praise.

***Try it. The results are amazing!***

***Remember***

*People learn for different reasons*

*We teach children, not swimming*

*We are psychologists first, technicians second*

*Your pupils say it all - watch the body language*

*The rewards are great for those who open their eyes!*

# Index

Further Reading — Published by

| | | |
|---|---|---|
| Harrison | "Teach your child to swim" | Usborne |
| Cregeen and Noble | "Swimming games and activities" | AC Black |
| ASA | "Introduction to Swimming Teaching and Coaching" | ASA |

**Addresses** (at the time of writing)

- (For awards and books) ASA Merchandising, 1 Kingfisher Enterprise Park, 50 Arthur St, Redditch, Worcestershire B98 8LG Tel: 01527 514 288 Fax 01527 514 277
- (For education and other enquiries) ASA Education Department, Harold Fern House, 18 Derby Square, Harold Fern House, Derby Square, Loughborough, Leics LE11 0AL Tel: 01509 618 721 Fax 01509 618 701

**To order more copies** of this book, or its companion volumes, please send a cheque with the slip below. You get a discount if your total order is for 10 books or more. Prices include postage and packing.

**Total** no. of books

1 - 9 .................................. £6.50 each
10 - 29 .................................. £5.50 each
30 - 99 .................................. £5.00 each

Send to: Anne Eakin, 48 Carpenters Wood Drive, Chorleywood, Herts. WD3 5RJ.
Tel: 01923 284 522 E-mail: rsaeakin@aol.com

...✂.............................................................................................................

Name and address for delivery: ------------------------------------------------------------------

(Please write clearly) ------------------------------------------------------------------

------------------------------------------------------------------

------------------------------------------------------------------

| | | No. required |
|---|---|---|
| **The Non-Swimmer** | *getting them started* | |
| **Swimming** | *teaching early practices* | |
| **The Competent Swimmer** | *teaching more advanced practices* | |
| | **Total books** | |
| | **Amount enclosed** | £ |

*Cheques payable to A. Eakin, please. Thank you for your order*

## About the Author

Anne Eakin has taught swimming at all levels for more than 30 years, and has trained large numbers of people to teach swimming to ASA standard. She lectures in the UK and abroad, and is a regular conference speaker.

She is an ASA Principal Tutor, designs attainment targets for the National Curriculum for use by local education authorities, and delivers In-Service Educational Training.

Anne published "Swimming - an illustrated guide to teaching early practices" in 1992, and "The Competent Swimmer - an illustrated guide to teaching further practices" in 1994, which many will find useful companion volumes.